# Table of Contents

*This book is dedicated to*

- Gabrielle Ashley and Victoria Marie

- Monica Lara

- Dulce Angela and her husband John Clement III

- All of our readers, many thanks for your time.

- God Bless all of you!!

# *What Is A Home?*

A home is a special place
where strong leaders are born and bred.

A home is where you are fed,
body, mind and soul.

A home is where you are safe and secure,
protected from all harm.

A home is where you can rest
to renew your strength and spirit.

A home is where you are healed,
not just your wounds but also your heart.

A home is where you are forgiven
and relieved of past mistakes.

A home is where you are loved
and accepted for who you are.

So, when you are out there striving to do your best,
do not get discouraged because
you can always come home.

- Victor Ronald, 1997

# *The Gift of Love*

Admittedly my effort
to put a hold on how I feel
is hardly any effort at all,
      love has taken hold
            of any sensibilities I had
                or given me.

Did I really once look at you
        as a friend?
Oh, you are, but so much more!

I hope my trusted friends
of long standing and seniority
will understand why I've become
to them a missing person.

If they come upon me now
I'm sure they'd find me certifiable
for any institution they could name.

- Laurel Richards

# *Ode to a Princess*

Take my hand, my love
As we gaze upward into
The starlit heavens.

My heart is stirred
By the majesty
Of this window to the universe
Reflected in your eyes.

Walk with me
In the calm of night
The serenity broken only
By a rustling breeze
Softly touching your hair
And making it glisten in the moonlight.

Tell me about our future
As I listen to your voice
Flowing like silk, reassuring me
With shared dreams and secrets.
Strengthening me with the promise
Of true friendship
And unending love.

- Carlos Rodrigo

## *Second Chance*

The little plant is almost gone
Most of its green leaves withered
By the spreading tree overhead
Which robs it of the sun
And by crushing canine paws
That tread indiscriminately.
Seeing its desperate state
The gardener retrieves it from the ground
Before it further diminishes
And only crumbling sprigs remain.
In a modest pot, blessed now
By the sun's warm, unrestrained eye
The plant's struggle to survive
Is replaced by a keen urge to grow.
In days it merrily sprouts
New foliage, twinkling bright green
To the delight of its rescuer.
The inner fire bursts forth soon after
As it sends its scarlet blossoms skyward
Rejoicing.

- Carlos Rodrigo

## *Renewal Song*

Your call awakened me
On that bright July day
And chased away the shadows
As your song began to play.

The chorus, ringing through the ages
Your melody of love that stirred
And set my heart free from its shackles
To soar as an unfettered bird.

And in the years I've felt out of tune
You brought me back, giving me a voice
To sing in harmony, with your plan
And in every circumstance rejoice.

So your song plays on, reviving
My spirit with your love's first call
As the rain waters a thirsty earth
You fill me, my all in all.

- Carlos Rodrigo

# *The Struggle*

Only I can feel the dark, murky waters
raging deep within my soul.
Only I can understand the pain
and guilt which makes my life whole.

Only I appreciate all of
my experiences, good or bad.
Only I can feel the biting cold of
the mem'ries, which make me sad.

No one else can fathom
the depth of my mind and thoughts.
For only I can bear the scars
of all the battles I have fought.

It is I that constantly struggle
to be no one else but myself.
No one else can fight this war
that I wage against no one but myself.

No one can really understand.
Even at the very least.
All the pain that I have to bear
to avoid releasing the beast.

Through all these things
Only I can choose.
Either to fight or win.
Or to surrender and lose.

- Victor Ronald

# *Reflections from a Year-Old Wedding Cake*

Today, my sister Dulce celebrates her first year of marriage. Some sort of tradition required her to keep part of the wedding cake in frozen stasis, to be consumed by her and her husband when they hit this milestone. The cake has been sitting in my freezer for exactly one year, and since they live on the West Coast, she asked my younger sister Monica and me to stand-in for her and partake of the celebratory confection. I, being the best man and Monica, the maid-of-honor, we dutifully and bravely assented.

The week before this event, Monica and I traded jokes about the possibilities of food poisoning. To think of it, Dulce is actually one of my insurance beneficiaries, and it seems like a no-lose situation for her. She doesn't have to eat stale cake, and if it was worst than stale then she still gets something from it!

Jesting aside, I was unprepared for the sight of the cake when it was brought out. It made me realize how petty all the concerns about freezer burn and food poisoning were, and why certain traditions have special meaning. Looking at the cake brought a flood of memories connected to the event, which forever changed the structure and depth of my family. No pastry had ever evoked such a fascinating sense of nostalgia, so permit me to share some of the memories.

Years before the event, I would have long talks with my sister about marriage, delayed gratification, and the essential qualities of a husband. I recall all the hours of counseling that they undertook to prepare for their life together, and how they go through the disagreements and disappointments along the way. There were long phone conversations as they both struggled to finish school, and sleepless nights with the new baby that made my sister seem superhuman. Then there were the moments of lively banter between myself and a stranger, who would become a friend and a brother-in-law.

The years passed quickly and John and Dulce both graduated and set a date for the day. Weeks flew by, with many visits to the craft store and the dressmaker. There was tension about the guest list and the song list, and even the IOU list made the rounds to wreak havoc during the delicate time. Then someone suggested that the wedding party learn ballroom dancing, which led to hours at a college campus and in the living room, stepping on toes and kicking shins.

The weeks turned into days, with a wonderful bridal shower, and a livelier bachelor party along the way. The tuxedos for the groomsmen came, with the inevitable wrong sizes and returns. The wedding party got better at dancing, and no one complained of bruised toes after dance practice. A Sunday school room and a fellowship hall were clad in lavender, white and pink, transformed into a dance floor and reception area. The songs finally got past the censors and onto master tapes, and were just waiting to be played.

The day before the wedding, the men finally got their tuxes, much to the relief of the groom. The rehearsal came, and the wedding party was in a jovial mood. In response to the officious "Do you take this man to be your husband," the bride replied with a joking, "Well, uh, I dunno, I guess." The groom was equally guilty.

The big day came as a non-stop frenzy of activity. I can recall dozens of last-minute minutiae, from makeup to corsages to car decorations. The world did stand still long enough, for two people to share vows of everlasting love, before the tear-filled eyes of well-wishers and the smile of a heavenly Father. There were no jokes this time, only promises, full of passionate devotion and sincere determination, to care for each other until the passage from life to eternal light. I must ask them.

"Do you remember the words?"
The declaration of the union followed, with an exit down the aisle, and minutes of waiting as the photographers did their work. There was a joyous reception, with the obligatory toasts and introductions, and the much-awaited exercise in cake smearing and evasion. The dance floor

was opened and the songs began to play. The tender first dance was followed by a variety of music, and while the dancers took the center, the photographers and matchmakers did their work from the sidelines. I especially recall gliding along the dance floor, looking into a beautiful visage framed with long, red-gold hair...

The day had to end sometime, in a shower of birdseed and the clattering of soda cans. The gaily décor was taken down, the gifts whisked away, and the flowers swept from the floor. The silence of the church punctuated the absence of the newly married pair, off to celebrate like saints ascended to heaven, leaving certain mere mortals wondering and dreaming when their turn would come.

I can only assume that a husband and wife who eat this year-old wedding cake will vividly remember the day and events that led up to it. All anniversaries are special, but the first year has wonderful significance. Men were commanded in biblical time to spend their first year making their wives happy, which shows how valuable this time is to God. Taking the first year to build a lifetime of love, and celebrating it by remembering the very first day of oneness, is what the anniversary and the frozen cake signify. I believe God looks down from heaven and sees how forgetful we become, and so gives us reminders of his love in special events like these, to testify of His greatness and His glory, that we may give praise to the One who causes all things to grow and flourish.

These are my reflections from this year-old cake. John and Dulce, in contrast to the condition of the cake, I'm certain that your marriage has remained fresh, as God has caused your love to grow and flourish in this past year. And He will continue to do this, as you both remain united in His love. Congratulations and God bless you!

- Carlos Rodrigo

# Two

I went back to look for you
Not understanding the language of hello
I thought I'd speak it just the same.
I bathed.  Left the window open and one light on.

The heat was off and as we warmed each other
You made up for all those indifferent backs
That turned from me these many months

The clock was running down and I had taken no
        precaution for the coming night.
All the while your arms were disengaging,
Your smile receding and your touch not tender and
        not there.

        I'd forgotten that we were loving at your option
        Entangling at your convenience and
                elevating one the other
        Only just by your design.

Unprepared I was and am when any door
I thought I helped to open
        closes.
Especially while I look the other way.

- Laurel Richards

# Ode To Dreamers

There are certain people
with the very gift of creativity
    and a great gift of imagination
    resting on their fingertips.

They spin webs of magic
in their minds they see stars
    seeing things that most of us
    fail to discern.

Why do we lose our grasp
on the wildest fantasies
    spawned in our colorful, creative minds?
    Yet these we spurn.

I do not believe
that dreamers never succeed
    nor do they live
    in their own world of make-believe.

I feel as if dreamers
have the real grip
    on the wonderful reality
    or a horrible truth.

They are very fortunate
yet some see the gift
    as a blessing in disguise
    and others let it fly away.

- Carlos Rodrigo

# On the Eve of Battle

Dear Lady –

Tomorrow's a reckoning indeed
    When foemen will contest
    This lonely king's field
    Victory means little
    For my soul is in your hands.

    My strength melts away
    At the sound of your voice
    Your lips calling my name
    Adding sweetness to my defeat.
    But sorrow grips this warrior tonight
    My dear lady, at the absence of you.

    I cry, for your cruel inattention
    Snaps the tender need of my affection
    Much like the Moon's heavenly beauty
    Reflecting cold light.

Am I an echo of a hurtful past?

    To think of love's injury to you
    Makes me burn to find
    That knave who sowed this deed.

    And bring to justice
    That knave upon sharp steel
    In clenched fist.

- Carlos Rodrigo

# Summer Love

I want to hold you in my arms, gently
Beyond sex and security, prestige and triumph,
to say once and for all, "I love you", and mean it
from the top of my head to the depths of my soul.

    This is the love that casts out fear
    that makes life worth living
    That takes a man and woman on earth
        and lifts them finally
    Above every power or pain that could wound them.

I have seen so many sights
    heard so many sounds
        but none as beautiful

As the sight and sound
    of a man and woman

Who say with their every act
    their eyes and all their being
        "I love you!!"

- Laurel Richards

# Nine Months

love is to sex

sex is to sin

sins are forgiven

so let's begin

3 hours of pleasure

9 months of pain

2 hours in the hospital

and a baby to name

father's a bastard

mother's a whore

none of this would have happened

if the rubber wouldn't have tore

- Laurel Richards

# The Twelve Days of Christmas

Day One:

> I fly with you between the covers
> As easily as among the clouds
>
> You transport me, you carry me
> To a world where dreams become reality
> And sadness never shows its many faces.
>
> I wonder if it's because
> Our hearts always knew
> That love once begun will grow
>
> And certainty conquers all the hidden fears
> As sure as a quarter moon grows to its full bloom.

Day Two:

> I looked up and there you were,
> All my dreams and some I never dreamed,
> Standing on what appeared to be
> Two good-sized feet.
>
> I celebrate your eyes because they looked at me
> Without restraint and no shame.
>
> Seeing you at my breath's edge filled
> My head with such a wonder
>
> I never got beyond your face,
> The smile that jumped from your lips
> And landed in your eyes,

The whole sudden experience took me by surprise
And I felt the fear pulling at my chest,
Insisting that you could never love me.

I wanted to push it all aside for once in my life
Jump across the room and take chances
I never took before,

I wanted to tell you all the things you wouldn't like
Before you had a chance to find out for yourself:

To tell you of a girl who only looks like a woman
Of an unshed tear that only looks like a smile
Of courage that only stands strong with trembling knees
Of small hands that finally could only be gentle
And of someone who whispers because you
                are too precious to lose.

I could only pray in silence that through your eyes
I would be what you watched
                closer to the woman you dreamed up the night before
Nearer to whatever you must have wanted or expected.

I have never known such gentleness as yours before,
Never knew that love could whisper with such quiet reverence.

Your courage frightens me, encourages me
I am now such fragility when once I was only strength

But then you would not have cared for me
Nor would I have seen your soul –

Only in weariness and desperation could
I have felt your love
And known a gentleness I have never known before.

Day Three:

> After all the years of running
>> and climbing mountains,
>>> I have finally come home!
>
> For years triumphs were enough,
>> but they did not consider my heart
> Which needed to give and receive
>> that which was reserved solely for you.
>
> There is the final mountain to climb
>> quiet nights by the fire
>> courage to face
>> the fears I avoided all my life,
>
> And I want you at my side and to be there for you as well.
>
> I cannot promise you more than I am,
>
> But I will be here with all I have to give
>> weary of illusions
>> tired of fantasies
>> sated with vain imaginings that ask
>> nothing and give little as well.

Day Four:

> Each day I will try to confront
>> what I avoided.
> To face life as it is and not as
>> I want it to be.
>
> I will find you even as I discover myself,
> I will find you with enough love
>> to nurture me back.

To courage and understanding,
            joy and energy,
And a future that sings with
            hope and passion.

I have been alone long enough
Docile and speechless, lost and afraid.

I expect no miracle, no lightning bolt or comet
Acclaimed in all the corners of the world.

I just want someone free enough to love and be loved,
To cling and to hold, to nourish and ask nothing

But love and commitment and mutual support
I have struggled long enough, prayed patiently enough.

Now I will reveal myself like a
            tree in all seasons
And love you, just love you, beyond
            logic and all reasons.


Day Five:

I did not know such love existed,
Gentle and fragrant beyond all words,
A dream I never hoped to realize,
Where souls speak and performances end.

God sent you into my life when all my patterns
Of blindness and needs have been established,
When I walked the same road again and again for love I never got,
When I chose some pseudo-strength that ultimately sought to
      control me and destroy my freedom,
When security became more important than life and love!

I thought life had no meaning, that there was only endless
emptiness, And I distrusted all.

All I know now is that love does exist,
That a day and night with you are worth all the pain,
And that the love that began so shyly, so cautiously,
Can last forever!


Day Six:

Why do I love you?

There are no words, only familiar smells
    and closeness beyond all reckoning
A gentle touch in the night, a quiet look of love
On a grey afternoon.

I never wanted perfection, only caring
Not striking beauty, but honest understanding
One who simply knows me and loves me for what I am

And has ceased to look for anyone else
Not because there is no time but no possible reason.

I still want to nurture and be nurtured,
    to care about each need
To be concerned about each pain and to know there is one

Who lives to make my days joyful,
    to bring my heart and hope alive
A voice that says nothing,
    a heart that asks nothing but my presence

I want a friend who understands, whose arm is linked with mine,
Whose vision penetrates, and words somehow touch my soul.

I see the tenderness of your mind
And send you nothing but love from a planet beyond our own.
You are my friend and lover.


Day Seven:

    No man ever held a woman
    the way that you hold unto me just now,
    or if one did
    I never heard about it
    not in a story book
        or at my ear.

    If it were so,
    if there were even one
    one experience the same as this
    on record or on file,
        surely I would know.

    Surely I would hear
    the celebrating down the street
    as someone else found out
    just how it is to be Columbus
    for the length of time
        that you're here.

    And all the while
    we thought we were different
    From what?  I wonder.

    Passion doesn't even need
        the wind,
    it is a need unto itself.

    Where friendship lurked
    now only truth dwells
    and silence between us
    will not come again.

Now we're altogether naked
even to the autumn trees
and yet more private
than we'll ever be.


Day Eight:

My credentials jangling in my jeans
are I know not enough
nor can my smile do all the work
unless some magic has happened in
        our eyes before.

Follow me
and I will lead you
through the darkened streets
        to home.


Day Nine:

Know that I'm a desperate woman
when in your arms,
more so when you're away.

I wind my watch when it needs no winding,
I puzzle harder puzzles
than my mind can comprehend.

By these simple acts
I manage for a time
to ward off facing
yet another confrontation
            with your absence.

I wish that you were home,
I wish that you were home for always.

I pray that I might never be
let down even once again.

I pray that we will
all reach home soon.


Day Ten:

Your eyes
are the bottom of the day
set on fire by words
made to move by sighs
and the rustling of desire.

Someday we are going to be lovers,
Maybe married
At the very least, an affair.

"What will I do when it happens?"
I used to ask myself.

What will I do
    now that it has?


Day Eleven:

For the quiet that
you've brought into my life,
the stillness
when you're here,

I bow to you
and know that you are my final love.
Final? Yes.

And I've no doubt
that as the drowned man
washed up on the shore

One day I'll be
beached as well.
To that direction
    I move then.

Unafraid.
Assuming that I'll have
yet another quiet night with you.


Day Twelve:

    You are your own answer
    Beyond books and seers
        psychics or doctors
    Beyond the strength that comes
        from what you've accomplished.

    Your weakness is as valuable as your strength
    Your helplessness is as lovable as your charm.

    You are God's child and each step of the way,
    He gives you bread and not a stone,
        food and not a serpent.

    All is part of the plan, as you look within
    And listen to the quiet persistent voice
        that tells who you are.

There is no strength greater than yours
No wisdom not available to you.

And love and light will flood your being

When you believe deeply enough to know
     that you are your own answer
In the beauty and creativity that make us all one.

Abandon anger and fear to the wind,
     sadness and pseudo-strength to the earth
     Be who you are, in whatever state and you will discover

That you are your own answer
In the silence of your heart
     where all light and power dwell forever.

- Laurel Richards

# Historia de un Amor

She sat at the Dulles Airport waiting lounge, thumbing through a Travel Magazine, her jet-black hair flowing like a tousled mane over her shoulders. At first glance, she looked like an eighteen-year old out on her first date, with an immaculate peach summer dress and a pair of white sandals. Looking closer, one saw a mixed innocence in her doe-like brown eyes and the quiet reserve of a woman who knew her place in the world.

Laura smiled at the thought that it would just be minutes away before she saw him. It seemed like she was always waiting between airplane schedules and his numerous business trips. The possibility of her being stranded was always there – business possessed him like a demon – and oftentimes he would call from overseas to tell her that his arrival would be delayed as the business negotiations were taking a little longer. Ian always seemed on edge when he made those calls, the impatience in his voice apparent as he always ended the call with "I miss you and I'll be hurrying home to you."

And she would laugh and say, "Don't worry – I'll always wait for you no matter how long it takes!"

And this was why Ian loved her so. Laura never complained about the long absences. If ever she got bored when he was away, he knew that she would always find something productive to do. And that she would always be faithful. The wounds from his first marriage with Sue had never healed; he never got over the sad experience of a philandering wife who went to bed with his friends whenever he was out on business trips. He vowed he would never get married again until he met her, during one of his business trips to the Orient.

At the thought of their meeting, she smiled, the pleasant memories giving her some joy and taking the dreariness of the airport lounge away a moment. She had her own career back then: a fast track, woman executive who was considered tough-minded and creative by her management peers. She did not have time for love, was disappointed by her own marriage that did not work so she poured all her energy into her career. Raised by a conservative family who did not believe in divorces, her unhappiness with her eight-year marriage found its release in her work for the family business. And that was how she met Ian – she was managing a conference for foreign executives who wanted to do business with her family.

Their meeting, on the first day, was uneventful. He got into the conference room with his colleagues and his Managing Director. He had just come from a series of business trips around Asia and Manila was their last stop. He took the seat at the head of the table with his Managing Director and proceeded to negotiate with the other country representatives from Singapore, Thailand and Malaysia. They were discussing a regional project that was to expand the communications links between the ASEAN countries and the Middle East.

Laura never got a full look at his face because she, herself, was busy taking notes for her own boss. Because the matter being discussed was confidential, the secretary was not allowed into the meeting room until she had transcribed and edited the minutes of the meeting. Head bowed in her task, she heard Ian's voice patiently negotiating with his business peers. She never forgot the sound of the voice, and looking back now, it was probably one she had always heard in her dreams.

When it was time to take the executives to lunch, Laura was approached by Ian and requested, politely, to order lunch to be brought into the room as he was set to do some last-minute changes to the proposals.

"And what would you like?" she asked.

"A cheese sandwich would be fine," he replied.

Unbelieving, she smiled and looked at the six-foot frame before her.

"A cheese sandwich?"

"Yes, please."

Hearing that answer, she replied, "All right. I'll make sure that you have a good dinner tonight to make up for the difference in calories!"

Ian chuckled at her, his blue eyes laughing. "And I'll make sure to sit beside you so that I'll enjoy the dinner!"

And true to her promise, she made up for dinner that night. The dinner was held in a plush, five-star hotel for all the executives, after which a show of dances and songs were rendered. All through dinnertime, Laura was only aware of Ian's presence at her side. They were seated at the far end of the dinner table, closest to the stage, and he concentrated his attention on her, talking about mundane things he had seen in his travels. She, in turn, translated the native songs into English for him. By the time dinner was over, they had become fast friends and had bridged the gap between their cultures. She was aware that their closeness was made possible by the seating arrangement, which was dictated by her manager. It seemed that Ian was an important figure in the project being discussed and her manager made every effort to please him.

Before they parted that night, he took her hand and kissed it goodnight. "I have never met anybody like you in my whole life," he said.

She brushed the remark gracefully aside, "I'm glad that you liked the dinner arrangements and the wine, you have suddenly become more gallant."

"No I am not drunk," he replied. "Only glad that I have finally found you." With this remark, he stared deeply at her dark brown eyes and wished her a good night's rest.

Laura was puzzled by Ian. Apparently, he was very bright and was respected by his colleagues. And yet, she sensed some sadness in him. As she prepared for bed that night in her hotel room, she thought, it's probably only because he is tired from his trip and the wine has affected him. Weary from the day's events and aware that she still had four long days ahead of her, she soon fell into a deep sleep.

The next morning, Laura got up to a bright sunshine flooding through the sheer curtains. She threw her robe around her shoulders and strode to her private hotel terrace to look at the view. The hotel swimming pool lay six floors beneath her room, and looking down, she saw Ian's handsome body swimming long laps across it. She watched him, amazed that he could be down in the pool at half past six in the morning, doing his laps and apparently getting a good dose of exercise. He swam for a good half-hour before he lifted himself out of the water. She was mesmerized by his whole appearance, his physique was even more striking when he was half-naked, and embarrassed by the obvious pleasure she took in seeing him without his knowing it, she retreated into her bedroom before he became aware of her.

Laura quickly got into the shower and dressed in her business clothes. Somehow getting into her tailored suit seemed a relief. You have to remember, she scolded herself, he is just a business associate. She then dialed her home phone and called her husband, "Hello, dear. How are you this morning?"

"Oh, all right. I'll be working late again tonight, and I'll be busy all day at the office so we can probably get in touch tomorrow. I'll take you out to lunch, if you have time."

"I don't think that's possible," she answered. "The conference will finish by Friday and we will probably be getting the documents ready by tomorrow. How about doing it next week?"

"Well, we'll see." Philip replied. "Somehow we'll work it out in our schedules when you get home on Saturday."

Hurrying into the documentation room to check on the work being done by secretaries, Laura saw the beautiful bouquet of red, scarlet roses on her table. How lovely, she thought.

Her manager never ran out of ways to complement her good work. She picked up the card that came with the flowers and, reading the message her face beamed. The card said, "You are doing excellent work, lovely lady. But I wish we had more time for each other." And the card and flowers were from Ian. What a thoughtful man, she mused. Not only a good negotiator but a good morale-booster as well!

The next four days seemed to fly. But it never went by without a present from Ian. A box of chocolates came on the third day and a witty card on the fourth day. Laura knew that she had made a very good impression and that he liked working with her. And each morning as she woke up, she would see him swimming at the pool. Seeing him there always gave an assurance, it was almost a signal that the day will turn out well.

As the conference finally ended, he took her aside and said, "How about a drink for a job well done? My director flies out of here tonight but I will stay for another day. Would you care to join me for another dinner tonight?"

"Why not," she replied. "We've finished our work and my secretary can wind up the details for me. Let me run to my room and I'll meet you at the bar by six o'clock."

At dinner that night, she found him amusing and well-traveled. He told her about his only son and she, in turn, told him about her marriage. It was comfortable being able to talk about her frustrations to someone she knew she would probably never see again. He finally opened up after an hour of conversation and told her that his marriage was not really all that well and that he was thinking of getting a divorce. As he talked about his wife's infidelities, she could see his blue eyes getting deeper and could read the hurt that she was causing him. "There are times when I know that I should have left her a long time ago. But I always look at my son and wonder who will raise him. And that always makes me stay."

Laura's heart went out to him as he said that. She reached across the table and took his hand, "Everything will work out fine. She will probably get tired of it soon enough and stop doing it. She also gets lonely when you are not around and that is probably the reason why she goes out."

She couldn't tell him of her own misery; her husband's blatant womanizing, his drinking sprees, and his cruelty to her when he got home drunk. She would sometimes get a fist and a slap when Philip did not know what he was doing. And if he wanted to stress his being a man, he would rape her after he inflicted pain on her. The man was cruel and mad, always making sure that the blows he inflicted on her were on her arms and legs, and can be covered by her clothes. And it did not matter if tears rand down her eyes when he assaulted her. He seemed to take pleasure in his being able to do as he pleased with her tiny body.

"You are not only lovely but understanding as well. But I'm afraid Sue will never change. I made a mistake when I married her."

"I will not argue with you on that," Laura replied. "But you are here and it is such a good night. Why don't we just enjoy the evening and forget about her?"

"Good idea," Ian beamed. "Let's do that."

And with that, their conversation turned to lighter things, and he recovered his own composure. The dinner went along marvelously, they moved on to the bar, had a few more drinks, listened to the band, and laughed with each other. It was an hour after midnight when they realized that time had lapsed so fast – and that they had to go into their respective rooms to rest.

"Will you take me to the airline office tomorrow to change my flight schedule?" Ian asked as they strode out the elevator on the way to her room. "I'm afraid staying for another day to be with you has made me miss my flight and I have to go there to personally to re-book it."

"Certainly," she said. "For such good company, that's a very small favor to ask. We'll go right after breakfast. Thank you for a lovely evening."

"It was a pleasure, lovely lady. Goodnight."

The next morning, Laura purposely strode down to the swimming pool and watched Ian do his daily exercise. She smiled at him as he jumped out of the pool, and reached for his towel to hand to him. He beamed at her, "So you're an early riser, too."

"Yes, I'm a morning person. And I've watched you at this pool for the past five days. I guess I shall miss you when you go."

"Don't think about that. We still have the whole day before us. Let's go and make the most of it, shall we?"

"That we shall. Let's have breakfast so I can show you some sights before I take you to the airport."

"Northwest Flight 401 now landing at Gate B." The announcement came by the airport speakers, jolting her out of her reverie. At last, she thought. Now I could give him my love!

She got out of her seat and positioned herself at the receiving gate. Ian never checked in his things if he could help it and he always traveled light. She knew he would be among the first passengers to cross the gate. Straining to get a glimpse of him, she soon saw his blonde, tall figure emerging, and her heart leaped. She would never get tired of seeing him home safe – how she loved him!

As soon as he saw her, Ian's face beamed. He broke into a fast stride, put his briefcase beside her little feet and gave her a long kiss. As he released her, he asked, "And how is my little American-Asian wife? Any mischievous pranks while I was away?"

"Nothing really. Just the usual boring things I do, mi amor."

"Now that is scary. Whenever you say that, I know that you have always started a big project."

"Ian, what a naughty thing to say! You have converted me from an honest, working woman to idle rich and you have the heart to tease me about it." She was always good-natured whenever he ribbed her about her projects. He was a good provider and she had never wanted for anything since they got married – but he allowed her to work at her charitable projects and, sometimes, even encouraged her to actively work for consultancy projects with companies. "I'll tell you about it when we get home."

On the ride home, Laura thought about how good this marriage has been. It was almost like a miracle...

She never thought about Ian again after he left her in Manila, one year ago. They kept in touch by letters, sometimes, but he had gone back to his family and she was resigned to her fate of being an ill-treated wife. Then one day, she received a letter from him telling her that his divorce was final and that Sue was getting custody of his only son. She knew then that she had to write him more often. He was in the middle of an important project, and she felt that he needed her emotional support.

So, she wrote him about her projects with deaf-dumb children and her work at the office, always sounding cheerful and positive. She never mentioned that her own marriage was getting worse by the day. A month after Ian's letter telling her of his divorce, Philip told her that he was leaving her for another woman. She cried then, out of pity for herself but also out of relief. She would never again endure the sleepless nights because of a marriage that was not working out.

Eight months later, Laura resigned her position from the family business, packed her bags and took up a scholarship that would take her to the United States of America. Before she left Manila, she wrote Ian about what happened to her marriage and gave him her address at the university.

Life in the USA was fun! It felt good to be near people who had no care but to study and take the world around them in a light-hearted way. Serious thoughts were acceptable, but the motto seemed to be, "Don't worry. Be happy!" She found new friends, started going out and meeting new people, and took in her new environment with a decidedly pragmatic approach. She even switched from dressing in her suits to blue jeans and tennis shoes. What a relief after years of being strait-laced!

One early morning, she found a letter from Ian in her mailbox. He was making a business trip to Virginia, in a city which was ten hours away by train from the university where she was studying.

"Would it be possible to see her?" he asked.

She couldn't believe what she read: that he would be at that place just when she would be attending a seminar in Washington D.C. – the coincidence seemed too good to be true! And that he wanted to see her! He gave her an address to reply to, if she wanted to see him. And that night, she wrote back:

"Yes, I would love to see you as I will be around the same area when you come here. We should have some interesting stories to tell when we see each other. I look forward to seeing you."

On that first night that Laura and Ian saw each other, they took a walk to a nearby restaurant, found it closed and decided to walk back to the hotel and order room service. When they got to his hotel room, Ian turned to her as he closed the door behind him and said,

"I dreamt about you. The only thing that kept my sanity all through my difficult divorce was the thought of you and your gentle smile. You were always there with your letters and I found the strength to carry on because I know you cared for me while I was thousands of miles away."

He cupped her heart-shaped face in his palms and started kissing her face. She couldn't move and tears started streaming down her cheeks.

"Don't cry, please," he whispered as he led her to the canopied bed. "I have been in love with you from the first moment that I saw you. And there was nothing I could do but wait for this moment with you."

Laura felt his strength, his gentleness and his love, as he took her in his arms that night. The next morning, rays of sunshine were streaming gently through the room when, half-awake and not certain that this was a dream, she felt Ian's kisses softly cover her body. She heard him whisper, "Good morning, my special lady," as he proceeded to embrace her. And then she was certain that Ian's presence was not a dream.

The first thing he did, for the next few days, was to make love to her as soon as the sun rose and in the evenings before he slept. Laura basked in the glow of her newfound love! She enjoyed each moment that they had for the next two weeks as they talked about everything they could think of. And, when it was time for Ian to go back to England, she felt apprehensive and sad.

"You will wait for me, will you?" he asked while she watched him packing his suitcase.

She looked at him, "Of course, as long as it takes," and she turned her face away so that she could not see the tears brimming in her eyes. "Now, finish packing, or you might miss your flight."

He took that remark as a jest, "So you still remember what I did a year ago. I would like you to know that you were the first woman who made me miss my flight."

"And I will probably be the only one you will always fly home to, in the future." She turned her back on him as she slipped a poem to his calendar book. "Please don't read the note until you are airborne." In it she had written this poem, to show how much she appreciated his love:

"I fly with you between the covers as easily as between the clouds
You transport me, you carry me to a land where dreams become reality and nightmares cease to exist."

The car rounded the driveway to their small chalet by the lake. Ian loved to go walking along the lake with Laura, with his left hand on his pocket and his right arm entwined around her tiny waist. He thought that buying this property would give him enough time to enjoy his hobbies, but business matters seemed to be taking more and more of his time lately. The walks around the lake were now hurried, each lasting less than what he would normally do. So, she thought of getting him another present, and this she wanted him to have on his next birthday, which was a week away. And so while he had been away on this business trip, she was quietly going around, shopping for his next present.

"What are we having for dinner?" Ian's query startled her and took her out of her reverie. "The food in the airplane was terrible and I couldn't wait to get home to your cooking."

She smiled to answer his question. They both knew what the answer to that one was. Oftentimes, their love for each other enabled them to think alike and anticipate each other's needs. Getting down from the car, they walked up the path to the house with their hands entwined, admiring the roses that lined their way.

He turned the key in the latch, twisted the doorknob and flicked the hallway lights on, after pushing the door open. After putting his bag and coat inside the closet, Ian looked around and marveled at the way Laura kept the house neat and tidy. She may be doing a million other chores, but she always managed to have the time to fix the house, especially for him. When he walked into the kitchen, the aroma of baked lasagna filled his nostrils. A wide grin flashed across his face.

"My favorite!" he exclaimed. "I don't know how you always manage to guess what I want. I was just thinking about this as I was changing planes in Los Angeles. I saw an ad for a great Italian restaurant they just opened – and which we are going to the next time that we are there – and it made me immediately remember your lasagna. Nobody makes it better than you, dear."

"Stop your praises or I'll think that you've been up to some very naughty things while you were gone," she parried his remarks.

She was always uneasy about her cooking, not quite wanting to believe that she was really good at it. It was one of the things she was not really fond of doing, but nonetheless had to do these days, when he was not around to take her out. Ian loved dining out, in fact loved showing her off to his friends. He was proud of the things she could do and marveled at the way she always handled herself in public. She had such a flair for clothes, always picking out what would complement her figure and color. Sometimes, he would catch her looking like a million bucks, and enjoying the sight, would remark,

"I think that you have been saving your money again. Why don't you do some shopping tomorrow and get some new jewelry to go with your new clothes? You always look better in new clothes, and I've seen you in this outfit at least four times."

Laura would always smile sweetly and say, "If you want me to."

His generosity with his money always touched her. She remembered how she had asked him if she could wear jewelry when they first met in Manila, and how amused he looked at hearing the question. Little did she know then that he owned stocks in several firms and had investments, which were paying off good returns. When they got married, he provided for her every wish. He would get her a new car without asking her for it; a new coat or handbag would always be standard presents from his out-of-town trips; and she had a perfume collection any woman would envy. If she so much as wished for a stuffed toy, he would find one in the airport lounge and carry it home to her.

And this was such a welcome change – her first husband had been very stingy with money, preferring to spend it on his vices and his friends than on her. There were times she could remember that she went to work with only a sandwich and a few pesos in her pocketbook, because Philip had run up so many credit card bills and was not making enough to pay them. Almost two-thirds of her salary went to his bills and she had barely enough to buy her own needs. Her own family was not informed of this, she kept it to herself, until the day they separated and when she filed for the divorce. By then she was so emotionally relieved that she even forgave him all his past transgressions, just as long as he kept far away from her and never saw her again.

After clearing away their dinner dishes, Laura remembered that she had to go out and make arrangements for Ian's birthday present. What excuse would she give him now, she wondered.

"Darling, would you like to take a nap while I pick some things up from the food store?" "As a matter of fact, I would love to," Ian replied. "Will you be long?"

"No, not very much.  I will surely be back in about an hour."

"All right, be careful driving now.  It's Friday night and there are so many drunk drivers in the streets tonight."

"Don't worry, I have nine lives," she jested.

Laura felt good after she got out of the lawyer's office.  The legal papers for Ian's boat had been ready for her signature when she arrived, and the meeting had lasted less than an hour.  She felt certain that he would like "Sara", a streamlined black beauty, when he found her on the docks next week.  She even conspired with David, her lawyer, to coax her husband out to the docks on the pretext of a complicated legal issue – so that the surprise would even be better.  Now she looked forward to getting home, jumping into the Jacuzzi with Ian and making passionate love to him.  Life was good and she was not about to let one moment of this life pass by without his knowing that she loves him!

As she fumbled for her car keys while standing on the curb, her eyes caught sight of a red Mustang parked across the street.  Beautiful car, she thought.  Must be owned by one of the yuppies in town for the weekend.  Somehow these cars were almost always owned by very rich, spoiled brats or yuppies who have a flair for fast cars.  Rarely did accomplished executives like her husband spend time with them, they preferred Volvos and Benzes.

She got into her car, turned the engine on, adjusted her mirror, and was about to pull off the curb when a man's face leaned over her car window and his hand tapped on the glass.

"Pardon me, but I saw you admiring my red car.  Will you allow me to take you for a spin?"

Laura turned around to see a pair of intense green eyes studying her.  He looked very disheveled in blue jeans, with a shadow of an unshaved beard. She thought him impertinent to even ask her that question – did he think that she allowed herself to be picked up from the streets?

"Thanks for your kind offer, but I've got to be somewhere within the half hour," she replied. "You do have a beautiful car and I hope you enjoy your weekend."

Three traffic lights later, she saw two beams flash bright on her rear-view mirror. She glanced back and saw the red Mustang following close behind her, blinking its headlights. She was annoyed at this intrusion. The fool, she thought. Not only a spoiled brat but persistent as well. She stepped on her accelerator pedal and weaved in the traffic, hoping to lose the car behind her. If she could only lose him before she got to the private access road to her house, then she would feel safe. But the more she sped, the less distance she put between herself and the other car. The Mustang dogged her every move and would not let her out of sight.

Laura felt panic slowly rising inside her. She had never before engaged in road racing. Although she was a skillful driver, she knew the approach to her house was through a winding road with steep curves. At the speed that she was driving, her car would never take the curves and the possibility of her slamming into one of the trees, in rounding a curve, was almost a certainty. She had fifteen minutes before she takes that road and she had to think fast. With a determined move, she picked up the car phone. But before she could dial for Ian, the Mustang overtook her car and cut off her approach. Then it slowed down, forcing her to do the same, and as the two cars reached a deserted part of the highway, the lead car's driver slammed on the Mustang's brakes.

Laura slammed on her own brakes, to avoid a rear-end collision. The next thing she saw what the figure of a man emerging from the driver's side and striding towards her car. She quickly locked her doors. The man got to her car window and sneered,

"My little chickadee thought she could fly, huh? You're mine, baby, and no car can take you away from me!"

She could smell the alcohol from his breath – it was more pronounced now, than minutes ago, when he first offered her the ride. The man started to reach his hand through the window and, as soon as he did this, Laura pushed the automatic window button to trap his hand. Her assailant jerked his hand away from the window and almost lost his balance. He glowered at her and shouted,

"You bitch! Get down from the car this instant or I'm going to blow your brains out!"

As the man started to reach inside his jeans jacket, Laura threw her car in reverse, swerved to avoid running over the man, then sped forward into the night. Her body was shaking like a leaf as she reached for the car phone and dialed for Ian...

The bright sun hit Ian's eyes as he walked up the hill with a bouquet of red roses for Laura. He had just come from a meeting with David, his wife's lawyer, and he carried in his shirt pocket the deed to "Sara" – which David described in glowing praises.

"You'll never believe how beautiful she is until you see her!"

And as if the gift was not enough, Laura had enclosed one of her favorite poems – just for the birthday. It read:

"Let not love claim itself to be true
Instead let it be as the Bible stands
Holding out in the senseless void
Ridiculed yet complete.

Let not love claim itself to be eternal
Instead let it be as the green grass
Drying up yet still alive
Never conquered by summer's heat.

Let not love claim itself to be perfect
Instead let it be as a diamond
Pressured and heated
Shining all the more.

Let not love claim itself to be unyielding
Instead let it stand as a mountain
Weathered and beaten, never falling
Even if it is reduced to a hill.

Let not love claim its purity
Instead let it be the rain
That falls upon the dirty earth
Washing away all the grime.

Let not love claim the brightness of its light
Instead let it be as God's love
Which shines more than a thousand suns
And which is light itself.

And let not love claim to be all of these
Instead let it be like my love for you."

Ian could never remember a time when his wife didn't try to please him. She always tried to make him happy. One only has to look to see that her one best trait was that she always thought of others before herself. And if she could make a difference by doing something extra special to help make someone happy, she would do it – even if it meant she had to sacrifice a small part of herself.

He reached the top of the hill and felt a lump on his throat. How many times he wished he could be by her side, while he was travelling on business. He wanted to have the time to tell Laura how happy he is with her, take her to the foreign places she had always wanted to see or take her driving around in the sun in her car – to see her black hair flying in the wind. Laura meant everything to him and, finally, he was going to have the time to be with her because he would not be traveling for at least five years. He was glad when he got the news of re- assignment to the head office – and couldn't wait to break the news to his wife when he came home. He had a bottle of champagne and a beautiful emerald necklace waiting for her that night she had to run out for an errand after they had dinner.

And now – there she was – sitting on a wheelchair at the top of the hill. Ian took a few steps, and then knelt to place the bouquet of red roses on her lap. He looked into her eyes to find a response – but her eyes continued to stare at the distance. He never understood what happened that night and the police couldn't give any explanation, either. They had found a red Mustang smashed into a tree, wrecked beyond recognition. The police said that the driver lost control of the car as it rounded a curve and then went crashing into the trees.

Laura was in shock when they found her, a tiny hand clutching the small pistol Ian had begged her to keep in the glove compartment. The police said that she attempted to escape her assailant by running into the forest. She had not gone far when she twisted her right ankle. But no bullets were fired from the gun. Laura must have waited, in terror, until she heard the red Mustang crash into the trees. Ian took her to the hospital after the police escorted her home. The doctors did not find anything wrong with her, except the broken ankle, and they advised Ian that she needed a lot of rest. His beautiful wife, once so full of life, now sat staring in the distance. She never talked about what happened – in fact, she turned away from Ian whenever he started to question her about it. Ian bent to give his wife a kiss on the forehead, and said,

"I will always wait for you no matter how long it takes."

Laura looked at her husband, smiled as she took the bouquet from him, and simply said," I love you, Ian."